MOUNT ZION:
in the FULLNESS
of HIS PRESENCE

Mount Zion:
in the Fullness
of His Presence

*The Mystery of the
Tabernacle of David*

Ann Tankesley

XULON ELITE

Xulon Press
2301 Lucien Way #415
Maitland, FL 32751
407.339.4217
www.xulonpress.com

Paperback ISBN-13: 978-1-66282-922-2
Hardcover ISBN-13: 978-1-66287-777-3
Ebook ISBN-13: 978-1-66282-923-9

Table of Contents

Many thanks to my life-long friend, Tanna Griggs-Finley, who so kindly sacrificed time to read my manuscript several times, and to Faith Luttrell for her support.

This book is dedicated to my daughters, who have been through fiery trials and come out even more beautiful.

Introduction

> It is the glory of God to conceal a matter; To
> search out a matter is the glory of kings. —
> Proverbs 25:2

The Tabernacle of David was one of the hiding places where God concealed glory. How do we know this? One clue was that the details which make up the revelation are scattered in isolated passages across several books of the Bible: 1 Samuel, 2 Samuel, 1 Kings, and 1 Chronicles. While some of the details are clearly stated for us, other details are implied. For example, 2 Samuel 6:13–18 and 1 Chronicles 15:1–29 describe in elaborate detail the ritual David followed over the course of one day when moving the Ark of the Covenant to the Tabernacle of David, but the Scriptures are silent about the appearance of the Tabernacle of David itself, the destination and home for the ark for many decades.

However, since the Bronze Altar, the Golden Candlestick, the Golden Altar of Incense, and the Veil of Separation in the Tabernacle of Moses were never moved to the Tabernacle of David (1 Chron. 16:37), it seems implied that the Tabernacle of David was not divided into the Holy Place (first inner chamber where the Golden Candlestick, the Golder Alar of Incense and the Golden Table of Showbread were located) and the Holy of Holies (the inward most chamber where the Ark of the Covenant was located). On the other hand, one can surmise from this as well as the public celebration involving 'all of Israel' as the ark was moved to Mount Zion that all worshipers at the Tabernacle of David had access to the presence of the Ark of the Covenant; access unheard of at the Tabernacle of Moses where only the High Priest on the Day of Atonement could pass through the Veil of Separation and gain access to the Ark of the Covenant in the Holiest of Holies (Lev. 16:31). Details in the Bible which are implied or are scattered in random locations are signs that God was concealing a matter.

The Tabernacle of David was a tent (1 Chron. 15:1) that David erected on Mount Zion (a hill in present-day Jerusalem) which became the resting place for the Ark of the Covenant

before it was moved into the temple. It was different from the Tabernacle of Moses because there was no Outer Court, Holy Place, or Holy of Holies, and the order of worship as reflected in Psalms was unlike anything the Jewish people had experienced up to that point. We also know that when the early church was debating what was to be expected of Gentiles who were joining the church, James stood up and quoted from Amos 9:11-12 about the Tabernacle of David being re-built so "that the remnant of men may seek the Lord and all the Gentiles who bear my name." Thus, James implied that the Tabernacle of David was more than a tent; it was an archetype for the church, an instructional role model for including the Gentiles in a covenant relationship with God (Acts 15:13-18). But Amos 9:13-15 goes on to reveal that the re-building of the Tabernacle of David would occur in the days before "the reaper will be overtaken by the plowman." So at the very least, the Tabernacle of David had to do with the last days, was a new form of worship, and was a model for the early church.

The Ark of the Covenant was a gold-covered chest with the statues of two cherubim on the lid. It was made according to a pattern that God gave to Moses and contained two stone tablets, a pot of manna, and Aaron's rod. The Ark of the

Covenant was located in the Tabernacle of Moses in the Holy of Holies. It was carried, along with the rest of the tabernacle, through the wilderness and into the Promised Land, where it was eventually removed from the tabernacle by the sons of Eli, the high priest, and carried into battle. Unfortunately, the ark was never to return. The Philistines captured it in battle and moved it from place to place, leaving a trail of death and curses in its wake, until it eventually ended up in the house of Obed-Edom. David moved it from that location to Mount Zion. During the ark's time of exile from the Tabernacle of Moses, the priests continued to offer sacrifices before the tabernacle, now an empty shell—devoid of the presence of God.

To keep the reader focused on what is important, I avoid repeating generally known parts of David's story not related to the Tabernacle of David. In this I assume a basic understanding of the Bible. For example, I assume that the reader knows that Samuel, who lived during the times of the judges, was dedicated by his mother Hannah to serve at the Tabernacle of Moses and who later became a prophet who anointed first Saul as king and then David. I assume that most know that Saul lost his right to rule because he made sacrifices he had no authority to offer and because he did not follow through with God's instructions on to how to handle the people he conquered and their chattel. I also assume that the reader knows that David, the youngest son of Jesse, was in the fields with his father's sheep when he was called to join his family gathering with Samuel and that he and his family were all taken by surprise when Samuel anointed him as king.

DAVID'S ANOINTING

1 Samuel 10:1: "Then Samuel took a flask of oil and poured it on Saul's head..."

1 Samuel 16:13: "So Samuel took the horn of oil and anointed him (David) in the presence of his brothers, and from that day on the Spirit of the Lord came upon David in power."

Luke 1:69: "He has raised up a horn of salvation for us in the house of his servant David (as he said through his holy prophets of long ago), salvation from our enemies and from the hand of all who hate us--to show mercy to our fathers and to remember his holy covenant."

Psalm 18:2: "He is my shield and the horn of my salvation, my stronghold." This Psalm is attributed to David[1].

Psalm 89:17, 20–21: "For you are their glory and strength and by your favor you exalt our horn. Indeed, our shield belongs to the Lord, our king to the Holy One of Israel. Once you spoke in a vision, to your faithful people you said: I have bestowed strength on a warrior; I have exalted a young man from among the people. I have found David my servant; with my sacred oil I have anointed him. My hand will sustain him; surely my arm will strengthen him..." This Psalm is attributed to Ethan the Ezrahite.

At the time of David's anointing by Samuel, in the midst of that momentous and unexpected event, Samuel pouring oil from a horn must have seemed like an insignificant

---

[1] Arguments as to the accuracy of the Psalm superscriptions presented in Gentry, P. J. (May/June 2021.) "Are Psalm Superscriptions Part of Scripture, or Are They Later Additions?" *Bible Study Magazine.*

detail. In contrast, when Saul had been anointed, Samuel had used a flask. But the availability of David's vessel required the sacrifice of a male animal, full grown and powerful, its horns a defensive weapon adorning the head of the animal like a crown, a symbol of its kingly authority surviving the death of the animal. The oil that Samuel poured out on David that day was poured from a horn, sanctified by a sacrificial death, a symbol of authority that transcended death, the original purpose of the vessel being that of a weapon. Saul's anointing, in contrast, was a more measured one. His anointing was poured from a manmade vessel. His kingdom was to be temporal, earthbound. The source of David's anointing, however, was based on a life laid down, a life whose authority was untouched by death: an eternal life.

That seemingly small difference between David's and Saul's anointing meant that David's kingship was different from that of Saul's. His line would "be established forever," as revealed in Psalm 89:4, and "his throne would last through all generations."

Before Samuel as a small child had shown the first signs of being a prophet, Samuel's mother, Hannah, prophesied about David's anointing. In 1 Samuel 2:10, she declared that God would exalt the "horn of his anointed" and "give strength to his king." In her prophetic statement, she tied together the words "horn" and "anointed," "king" and "strength." She knew that one day Israel would have an anointed king appointed by God and that her son would be involved. She knew the anointing would be sanctified by a sacrifice. She knew that this anointing would give the king power.

David may not have understood the significance of the horn when Samuel anointed him, but he later understood. In Psalm 18:2, David, under the inspiration of the Holy Spirit, declared the Lord to be "the horn of my salvation." With those words, David indicated that he understood that the horn was both God and the means of his salvation. But the revelation was not just given to David; others understood the implication as well. In Psalm 89:20-21, Ethan, one of the men assigned to sing praises before the Ark of the Covenant, later declared, "Once you spoke in a vision, to your faithful people you said: 'I have bestowed strength on a warrior; I have exalted a young man from among the people, I have found David my servant; with my sacred oil I have anointed him...'" The sacred oil that anointed David as king was associated with David's strength as a warrior.

"When a lion or bear came and carried off a sheep from the flock," David told Saul upon volunteering to confront Goliath, "I went after it, struck it and rescued the sheep from its mouth. When it turned on me, I seized it by its hair, struck it and killed it" (1 Sam. 17:34-35). In modern times, the Maasai hunt lions in groups of ten or more using spears and strategies honed by many generations, but whereas David, as a boy, alone and untrained, with only his hands and the simple items that a shepherd might carry, was fearless in confronting lions and bears. When Ethan said that God had strengthened David's arms, his words were not just poetic. They were literal. Ethan was saying that David had received supernatural strength and boldness through his anointing.

In Luke 1:69, Zechariah, upon encountering Mary, Joseph, and the baby Jesus in the temple, declared in a song that God would raise up a "horn of salvation for us in the house of his servant David." The horn was revealed in the song to be a person in the lineage of David, and Zechariah implied that the baby he was holding was that horn.

In Psalm 133, under the inspiration of the Holy Spirit, David declared:

How good and pleasant it is when brothers
live together in unity!
It is like precious oil poured on the head,
running down on the beard,
running down on Aaron's beard,
down upon the collar of his robes.
It is as if the dew of Hermon
were falling on Mount Zion.
For there the Lord bestows his blessing,
even life forevermore.

The anointing that David spoke of in Psalm 133 was not just about one that sanctifies and qualifies one man to be high priest; the solidarity of the oil as it rolled down from the head of the priest illustrates unity among God's people. In David's vision, it fell like dew on Mount Zion. It conferred eternal life.

Aaron lived a thousand years before David established Jerusalem as his capital and before the first mention of Mount Zion is found in Scripture. Under the rules for the priesthood in which Aaron received his anointing, priests were anointed individually. In other words, each anointing of the high priest sanctified only one person.

So, the original Aaron was the first man in a long line of men who were anointed as high priest. But the priesthood that David spoke of was different. His Aaron pointed to an anointing that fell like dew on Mount Zion and was like the people of God dwelling together in unity. Just as Jesus was called the second Adam (Rom. 5:12-19), David's Aaron was a second Aaron. The Aaron that David spoke of was, thus, a type. David's Aaron stood at the beginning of a new age and a new relationship between God and His people. Under the inspiration of the Holy Spirit, in Psalm 133, David revealed a new vision of God's people, one that associated the anointing of the high priest with unity among God's people.

But the role of a high priest in the traditional priesthood was solitary. He, the lone representative of all of Israel, appeared before the ark of God's presence. But contrary to this archetype, when this second Aaron was anointed, the anointing oil fell like dew on Mount Zion. The imagery of this archetype is consistent only if the high priest's relationship to Mount Zion was that of a covering; in other words, Mount Zion was under his authority. Only then could the anointing oil also fall like dew on Mount Zion. A line of authority with countless numbers of people not of Aaron's lineage implies a kingship. It is, thus, implied that this second Aaron was also a king.

In Psalm 110, David declared:

> The Lord says to my Lord;
>> 'Sit at my right hand
>> until I make your enemies
> a footstool for your feet.'
> The Lord will extend your mighty
>> scepter from Zion;
>> you will rule in the midst of your enemies.
>> Your troops will be willing
>> on your day of battle.
>> Arrayed in holy majesty,
>> from the womb of the dawn
>> you will receive the dew of your youth.
>> The Lord has sworn
>> and will not change his mind:
> 'You are a priest forever,
>> in the order of Melchizedek.'

Under the inspiration of the Holy Spirit, David saw in a short passage in Genesis a seemingly random encounter between a king of Salem and Abraham a revelation about the kingship of God's Messiah and his own kingship and role as king and priest. David had found one of the hiding places where God's concealed His glory.

Hebrews 7:1-17 says:

> This Melchizedek was king of Salem and priest of God Most High. He met Abraham returning from the defeat of the kings and blessed him, and Abraham gave him a tenth of everything. First, his name means "king of righteousness"; then also, "king of Salem" means "king of peace". Without father or mother, without genealogy, without beginning of days or end of life, like the Son of God, he remains a priest forever.

> Just think how great he was: Even the patriarch Abraham gave him a tenth of the plunder! Now the law requires the

descendants of Levi who become priests to collect a tenth from the people-- that is, their brothers-- even though their brothers are descended from Abraham. This man, however, did not trace his descent from Levi, yet he collected a tenth from Abraham and blessed him who had the promises. And without a doubt the lesser person is blessed by the greater. In this one case, the tenth is collected by men who die; but in the other case, by him who is declared to be living. One might even say that Levi, who collects the tenth, paid the tenth through Abraham, because when Melchizedek met Abraham, Levi was still in the body of his ancestor.

If perfection could have been attained through the Levitical priesthood (for on the basis of it the law was given to the people), why was there still need for another priest to come—one in the order of Melchizedek, not in the order of Aaron? For when there is a change of the priesthood, there must also be a change of the law. He of whom these things are said belonged to a different tribe, and no one from that tribe has ever served at the altar. For it is clear that our Lord descended from Judah, and in regard to that tribe Moses said nothing about priests. And what we have said is even more clear if another priest like Melchizedek's appears, one who has become a priest not on the basis of a regulation as to his ancestry but on the basis of the power of *an indestructible life* (italics added). And for it is declared:

> You are a priest forever,
> In the order of Melchizedek.

David, like Jesus, was from the tribe of Judah, his anointing as a high priest was also based on "the power of an indestructible life."

The first time David tried to move the Ark of the Covenant from its location in the house of Abinadab to Mount Zion ended badly even though his intention was to honor God.

Thirty thousand of David's chosen men accompanied the ark. It was set on a new cart, and David and all of Israel celebrated with all their might, singing songs and playing instruments. But they got it wrong. Toward the end of the journey, when they came to the threshing floor of Nacon, the oxen stumbled, and Uzzah reached out to steady the ark and was struck dead. David was overcome with a fear of God that day, according to 2 Samuel 6:9-11.

Three months later, David tried again, but this time, he wore a linen ephod, the garment that according to the rules of the priesthood given to Moses in Exodus 28:4 was only to be worn by the high priest. "The priests sanctified themselves", and the Ark of the Covenant was carried on the shoulders of the Levites. According to 2 Samuel 6:13, when those who had carried the ark had taken six steps, David sacrificed a bull and a fattened calf, and upon the arrival of the ark at Mount Zion, he sacrificed burnt and fellowship offerings, distributed bread and meat to the people and blessed them. This time, David got it right. While Saul had lost his right to rule because he had offered sacrifices that he had no authority to offer, David was not afraid to offer sacrifices and even wear the garment of the high priest in the presence of the ark: God's throne on earth. This was because David was following the vision God had given him: he had assumed the role of a priestly king, and God signaled His approval. This time, no one died. This time, a king retained his right to rule. David's anointing as a priest gave him the authority to offer sacrifices; a role that was outside Saul's authority as a king.

David sacrificed the calf and bull at a pivotal moment, at the beginning of a second attempt to move the ark —the second attempt necessitated because David had been careless the first time and a man died. He and his counselors chose them after a three-month deliberation, and only after they had scrutinized every detail involved in moving the ark. While a fattened calf is usually associated with a feast, here David did not even offer its meat in a ceremonial way for anyone to eat. And significantly, it was a king who sacrificed the fattened calf, its death witnessed by all of Israel. This implied that the message behind those sacrifices was of national importance.

A sacrifice in combination with celebration implied that the sacrifice was associated with a burnt offering: a life laid down in total obedience to God. Burnt offerings were accompanied by fellowship or peace offerings. Although the calf and bull offerings made at the beginning of the celebration are not identified as being burnt and fellowship sacrifices, since the celebration began after them, one must have been a burnt offering. So, the celebration that day began with a burnt and fellowship offering and ended with burnt and fellowship offerings at Mount Zion.

In Leviticus 1-3, the requirements for burnt and fellowship offerings are described with the burnt offering being either bulls, sheep, goats, or birds and the fellowship offerings being male or female adult animals from a flock or a lamb or goat. So neither the prescribed burnt or fellowship offerings allowed for the sacrifice of a calf as a regular burnt or fellowship offering. It is in Leviticus 9:3-4 that the full significance of the bull and calf being offered together are revealed. Here, Moses told Aaron and the elders to say to the Israelites:

> Take a male goat for a sin offering, *a calf* and
> a lamb—both a year old and without defect—
> *for a burnt offering* and an *ox* and a ram *for*
> *the fellowship offering* to sacrifice before the
> Lord, together with a grain offering mixed
> with oil. *For today the Lord will appear to you.*
> (italics added)

Leviticus 9:23-24 says:

> When they (Moses and Aaron) came out,
> they blessed the people *and the glory of the*
> *Lord appeared to all the people. Fire came out*
> *from the presence of the Lord and consumed*
> *the burnt offering and fat portions (fellowship*
> *offering) on the altar.* (italics added)

David's offerings of a bull and calf revealed that he was following an abbreviated version of a protocol that Moses had followed only once—on the day that the glory of the Lord appeared to Israel. It is implied that the animal from whose horn David was anointed provided the cleansing from sin while the calf provided the burnt offering, and the bull provided the fellowship or peace offering. But David's burnt offering was not any calf; his was a 'fattened' calf that had gone through a period of preparation. David's offerings were also sacrifices not associated with the daily, monthly and yearly sacrifices made in association with the Tabernacle of Moses by the Aaronic priesthood.

In the Scriptures, references to a 'fattened' calf are rare. Genesis 18:1–15 says Abraham served a 'flattened' calf to three visitors, one of whom was identified as being 'the Lord.' Afterwards, it says, the Lord promised, "I will surely return to you about this time next year and Sarah your wife will have a son." Thus, the 'fattened' calf was associated with the covenant promise to Abraham of a son. In yet another association with sonship, Jesus, in Luke 15:11–31, said in the parable of the prodigal son that the father served a 'fattened' calf to celebrate his son's return. So, on another level, the 'fattened' calf pointed to a celebration associated with a son's return to his father's house. Thus, David's sacrifice of a 'fattened' calf was a reminder of the covenant promise to Abraham of a son through whom "all peoples on earth" would "be blessed." But the sacrifice of a calf was also associated with the day the glory of God appeared to Israel. Significantly, the ritual David followed that day identified the 'revealing of God's glory to the people' with the covenant promise of a son.

The implication of David's gift of bread, which he made after the ark had reached Mount Zion, was startling. The words for bread, *lehem hallat*[2], used here are the same words

---

used in Leviticus 8:26 for the wave offering (a sacrifice that was waved before the altar) made when Aaron was ordained as a priest. While some of the bread was burned on the altar, the rest was eaten by the priests before the Tabernacle of Moses along with meat from the fellowship offering. This association means that the fellowship sacrifice David offered at Mount Zion was not one made by just any worshipper. By giving the bread, *leham hallat,* to the people along with the meat associated with a fellowship offering, he was implying that the fellowship and burnt offering were associated with the ordination of a priesthood and that, moreover, the people were part of the priesthood. But what is even more startling, since 2 Samuel 6:19 and 1 Chronicles 16:3 emphasized that both "men and women" were given a loaf of bread, David implied that both men and women were equally part of the priesthood with the women not just included as part of a priest's family.

While kings were anointed by oil, the ordination of the Aaronic priesthood required an anointing by oil and three sacrifices: one a sin offering, one a burnt offering and one a fellowship offering. In other words, the ordination of an Aaronic priest required revelation found in all three sacrifices. In the same manner, David's priesthood, being rooted in Jewish precepts, could also have required an anointing and these three sacrifices. A sin sacrifice by itself, as in the case of the Passover lamb, suggested the innocence of the one who dies for sin, while a sin sacrifice combined with burnt and fellowship offerings implied a sacrifice for sin that is innocent but whose life was willingly laid down for the end purpose of not just removing sin, but to establish fellowship with God. In order for a priest to fulfill his role as intercessor, he had to be able to enter into the presence of God, and nowhere in Judaism does one animal sacrifice met all three requirements.

If Samuel's anointing of David as a boy had by itself made David a priest, then Jesus would not have said that David, while on the run from Saul, had the right to eat the consecrated bread from the Tabernacle of Moses because he was hungry—implying that it was not because he was a priest (Matt. 12:3-7). Because if at that point David had been a priest, since his priesthood was greater than that of Aaron's and had authority over it, how much more right would he have had to eat the consecrated bread than that of the Aaronic priesthood? It is, thus, implied that the death of the animal that provided the anointing horn did not meet all of the offering requirements for a priest.

The animal that provided the horn for David's anointing could have been regarded as fulfilling some of the requirements for an ordination into the priesthood. Certainly, it met the requirement of a sacrifice for sin. It would be logical if the ordination of the two priesthoods, David's and Aaron's, required different animals, so the separation of the two priesthoods was clear. If true, the calf sacrifice seemed to imply that the appearance of God's glory and the ordination of David's as a priest were one and the same event. But the 'fattened calf' also flagged another difference between the priesthoods— David's priesthood was associated with sonship. Abraham's promised son was also God's promised son, and being a son of God implied that he had all the attributes of God.

Because the animals sacrificed at Mount Zion are not identified, it is almost implied that they were the same as those offered at Obed-Edom's house. And, certainly, the burnt and fellowship sacrifices David made at Mount Zion were tied to the ordination of the people into the priesthood because he distributed *lehem hallat* to them. Since the Veil of Separation was not moved to the Tabernacle of David, it can be assumed that all worshippers had access to the ark—a situation which would be outside the revealed order in Judaism unless the people were ordained as priests. What is apparent is that from that day forward the worship surrounding the ark changed, and this open worship lasted for that generation alone. In other words, David's generation—the generation present when these sacrifices were made— was the only generation to worship in the very presence of the Ark of the Covenant. David wore a literal robe and was anointed with literal oil, and so it is also possible that the sacrifices associated with David's ordination into the. priesthood, as well as those of the people, were also literal. And if the people were ordained into a priesthood, it was not that of Aaron's, thus, the ritual surrounding the Aaronic priesthood would not have been completely followed. The impression is given that the celebration that day began with burnt and fellowship offerings at Obed-Edom's house that completed David's ordination as a priest, while the burnt and fellowship offerings at Mount Zion completed the ordination of the people into the priesthood.

Since the fellowship offerings probably represented the Messiah and David in his role as the priest-king was a

foreshadowing of the Messiah, David's gift of meat and bread that were probably associated with the fellowship offering implied on one level that they were a foreshadowing of gifts given by the Messiah to the people. The Messiah was both the sacrifice and the one who sacrificed: He was both the bread and the flesh they consumed. David was an archetype for the Messiah who would lay down His life only once, thus, David was the only one who could offer the sacrifices at Mount Zion, the sacrifices offered only once and not repeated as long as the ark remained on Mount Zion. And since David was an archetype for the Messiah, his ordination into the priesthood would not have allowed him to eat the flesh associated with the fellowship offering or to consume a bread offering—none of which are not mentioned as having occurred with the calf and bull offerings at Obed-Edom's house.

The anointing oil David spoke of in Psalms 133 did more than just confer unity and eternal life to those on Mount Zion—the people received the same oil that the high priest received when he was ordained. The people of Mount Zion were more than priests: they were high priest and, thus, could enter into the very presence of the ark. David as high priest ushered the people into their roles as high priests when he performed the sacrifices at Mount Zion and distributed meat and bread to the people. He was, thus, the first of many. This implies that his ordination came before that of the people. The first sacrifices at the house of Obed-Edom must have completed the ordination of David as high priest, while the burnt and fellowship sacrifices which occurred later at Mount Zion completed the ordination of the people.

Like a master conductor, Paul, in his interpretation of the Melchizedek passages in Genesis and Psalms 110, paid as much attention to the silences—the absence of information— as to the words that were spoken. Melchizedek, he noticed, was "without father or mother" because his genealogy was not given. Melchizedek's sudden appearance in Scripture, Paul pointed out, conveyed the impression that he was "without beginning of days or end of life". Thus, Melchizedek was revealed to be "like the Son of God". He "remained a priest forever." He, Paul goes on to say, became "a priest not on the basis of a regulation as to his ancestry but on the basis of the power of an indestructible life." With the same artistry, the silences—the information not given—concerning the Tabernacle of David are pregnant with meaning. The horn that anointed David is like Melchizedek. There is no information given about the death of the animal that provided the horn. Thus, the horn appears to have no beginning and no end, and, like Melchizedek, conveys the impression of being "eternal". In other words, this sacrifice was slain from the foundation of the earth. In a similar manner, the sacrifices David made at Mount Zion are described as being 'burnt and fellowship offerings, without any reference to the animals sacrificed, as though they don't exist. With the ordination of this priesthood being based on an anointing by a horn that is eternal in nature and by sin, burnt and fellowship offerings that are offered only once and seem to have no grounding in the suffering of earthy animals, the impression given is that this priesthood must be greater than the Aaronic priesthood with its dependence on continual animal sacrifices.

But the words that describe the sacrifices at the house of Obed-Edom are more concrete. Those animals are identified as being a calf and a bull, and because they are identified, we are able to associate those sacrifices with the sacrifices made by Moses on the day God's glory appeared to the people and with the covenant promise of a son and are reminded that their blood was shed. Thus, David's ordination is associated with the glory of God appearing to Israel and David becomes an archetype for the Messiah who is an embodiment of God's glory. It was after Jesus had died that the eyes of his followers were opened, and they beheld the glory of the Father in him. However, David also represented the Messiah who as high priest is the first man to enter God's glory and the means by which others as priests can also enter. In other words, he is the one who brings the people into God's glory. But the sacrifices may have been more than symbolic. Just as Moses and Aaron offered sacrifices to cover the people so that they could behold the glory of God, David's sacrifices could also have been intended to cover the people so that they could behold the glory of God associated with the ark. In that case, David's ordination as high priest also revealed God's glory to the people, with the completion of the sacrifices at Mount Zion ordaining the people as priests, giving them the right to remain in the presence of God. And because the sacrificial animals are identified, we are reminded that this ordination was based on the shedding of blood. Thus, the emphasizes is placed on this priest being identified with the calf and bull sacrifices, because he represented the one who is the burnt and fellowship offering. He is the one who is a willing sacrifice for sin that is offered for the purpose of fellowship with

God. He is also the one who brings the blood into the throne room which opens the door for others to follow.

And just as Jesus did not ascend into heaven and assume the role of high priest until after he had been made perfect through obedience, David, as an archetype for the Messiah, could not enter into his role as high priest until after he had offered a burnt sacrifice. For Hebrews 2:10 says, "In bringing many sons to glory, it was fitting that God—should make the author of their salvation perfect through suffering." Hebrews 5:8 later adds, "Although he was a son, he learned obedience from what he suffered and, once made perfect, he became the source of eternal salvation for all who obey him and was designed by God to be high priest in the order of Melchizedek." In Hebrews 5:8, sonship is associated with a life laid down, a burnt offering, and the Melchizedek priesthood. Therefore, David's offering of a calf, associated with the promised son, as a burnt offering, is revealed to be foundational to understanding the Melchizedek priesthood. The implication of the sacrifices at Mount Zion, with their association with sonship, with the revealing of God's glory and with the priesthood implied that David, as an archetype for the Messiah, brought the people with him into those roles.

When Jesus hung on the cross, they placed "above his head" "written charges against him: THIS IS JESUS, THE KING OF THE JEWS" (Matt. 27:37). Thus, it is revealed that it was the King of the Jews who was the sacrifice for sin. The horn that anointed David was probably from a ram, which in the Bible is associated with kingship, the ram being the leader of the flock and crowned with horns. In fact, the Hebrew word for ram, *ayil,* is also used for ruler[3]. David's anointing from a ram's horn points to a promise that a king would be a sacrifice for sin. So the beginning of David's royal bloodline begins with an anointing based on the sacrifice of an animal that is associated with kingships and embodies a promise that a king would die. And David's royal lineage concludes with the fulfillment of this promise. The promise that a future king would lay down his life, which enabled David to be anointed, was so sure, that it was as though the sacrifice had already occurred, so David, and the people he brought with him under his anointing, were able to lay claim to promises that were based on a new and better covenant.

Solomon, an archetype for the resurrected Christ, was also a Melchizedek king-priest. 1 King 1:39 says "Zadok

---

[3] 352. ayil; https://www. Biblehub.com

the priest took the horn of oil out of the tabernacle and anointed Solomon." After a dream in which God promised to give Solomon a wise and discerning heart, he returned to Jerusalem, stood before the ark of the Lord's covenant, and sacrificed burnt and fellowship offerings. The animals sacrificed, like when David made the offerings at Mount Zion for the people, are not identified because to fulfill the heavenly type the blood of Messiah could only be shed once which symbolically occurred when David completed the requirements for his priesthood and the calf and bull are identified as having died. By not identifying the animals sacrificed by Solomon, 1 Kings 3:15 leaves the impression that the animals did not exist, but we understand that the requirement of sacrifices for Solomon to become a Melchizedek priest was met because this passage tells us the burnt and fellowship offerings were made. It is also in these passages that God fulfills his promise to David to make Solomon his son.

According to John 1:1, "In the beginning was the Word, and the Word was with God, and the Word was God." The Bible, from beginning to end, is the revelation of Jesus, with the Old Testament pointing the way to Messiah so when he came, those who knew the Law and Prophets would recognize him. In these passages the Old Testament adds to our understanding of the Melchizedek priesthood, mentioned only once by David in Psalm 110. Here we gain more insight into why it was necessary for John to baptize Jesus. The water represented death. Like David, Jesus's baptism was a promise that a king would die. God anointed Jesus through the Holy Spirit in the image of a dove and set him aside to become a Melchizedek priest, but Jesus did not assume the role of priest until after he had finished the work of the cross and had ascended with the blood into the heavenly throne room. After he had died, he, in the role of priest, presented his body as a sacrifice. So, Jesus died king of the Jews but not as a priest. It is also here that we understand that the Melchizedek priesthood involves sonship.

A Melchizedek king-priest could not fulfill his role as a heavenly king and intercessor unless he was a son of God. Because as a son of God, he would share the nature of God and could therefore understand the mind and heart of God and in sharing the nature of God have the authority to release God's will on earth. He was not a servant but someone who ruled with God.

With the shedding of the king's blood, the king being God's son and, thus, perfect, the law was fulfilled, and sin was removed. But the shedding of the son of God's blood did something more than remove sin — it also removed the barrier between Jew and Gentile by fulfilling the law. This enabled the Melchizedek king-priest to reveal God's glory by bringing all of humankind into the presence of God. Through this means the King of the Jews became Lord of all who believe with the removing of the barrier between the Jews and Gentiles. Therefore, when David, as an archetype, completed the sacrifices at Mount Zion, he, by faith, removed the barrier between Jew and Gentile. For this reason, David's kingdom included both Gentiles and Jews.

After the first attempt in moving the ark failed, trying to move the ark a second time must have been difficult for David. His life and those with him depended on his hearing and understanding what the Lord expected. At some point during the procession, 1 Chronicles 15:26 records a pause in which seven bulls and seven rams were sacrificed. Because seven is the number of completeness, the sacrifice likely represents special fellowship or peace offering as that expressed feeling of completeness and unity with God. The words imply a marriage had taken place. This was not just any procession:

it was a marriage procession, bringing the bride to her home on Mount Zion.

The lack of explanation surrounding the ceremony involved with the moving of the Ark of the Covenant to Mount Zion was probably intentional. There was to be a mystery surrounding the events of that day to ensure that no king or generation that followed attempted to emulate what was to be an archetype for the church.

Psalm 24:7-10, attributed to David, declares:

> Lift up your heads, O you gates;
> be lifted up, you ancient doors,
> that the King of glory may come in.
> Who is this King of glory?
> The Lord strong and mighty,
> the Lord mighty in battle.
> Lift up your heads, O you gates,
> lift them up, you ancient doors,
> that the King of glory may come in.
> Who is he, this King of glory?
> The Lord Almighty—
> he is the King of glory.

In this Psalm, David speaks of the moment that God's glory entered Mount Zion.

Psalm 26:8, also attributed to David, said:

> I love the house where you live, O Lord,
> the place where your glory dwells.

And in Psalm 27:4, David said:

> One thing I ask of the Lord,
> this is what I seek;
> that I may dwell in the house of the Lord
> all the days of my life,
> to gaze upon the beauty of the Lord
> and to seek him in his temple.

David described his feelings of joy at being in the presence of God.

While Saul was anointed only once by Samuel and later confirmed as king by the people (1 Sam. 11:15), David was anointed three times. On the day when David was anointed by Samuel, no one stood under his authority. Over time, men slowly began to gather under David's leadership, and later at Hebron, the leaders of Judah came to him and anointed him as their king. In doing so, they acknowledged him as their king placing themselves under his authority. The anointing still on David from Samuel was extended to those under him as the new anointing oil flowed.

As David's anointing spread to those under his authority, so too did his boldness and power. Thus, began the extraordinary transformation of a group of thirty or so men among the original four hundred "discontented and men in debt" who followed David into the Mighty Men. 1 Chronicles 11:11, 20 and 22 says that Abishai killed three hundred men during one battle, while Benaiah fought and overcame a lion and an Egyptian who was seven feet tall and Josheb Basshebeth killed eight hundred men in one encounter (2 Sam. 23:8). The battle of Pas Dammim was won by David after Eleazar remained in a field of barley after the rest of the troops had fled (1 Chron. 11:12.) The Mighty Men were emulating David's exploits. They were more than military leaders, their exploits so extraordinary that they could only be explained by a supernatural power, their strength like that of Samson's, and their valor similar to that of Gideon's.

Seven years later, "all of Israel" came to David at Hebron (1 Chron.11:1-4). David made a pact with the remaining tribes before the Lord, "they anointed David king over Israel;" and from there they marched in "unity" under their new king to Jerusalem, where they captured the stronghold that became the "Fortress of Zion, City of David" (1 Chron. 11:4-5). Other men began to show great exploits as well. In 1 Chronicles 20:5, Elhanan, son of Jair, who is not listed among the Mighty Men, killed Lahmi, the brother of Goliath. Later Jonathan, son of Shimea, David's brother, probably joining David after he had reached fighting age, killed a huge man from Gath with six fingers and toes on each hand and foot. David's third anointing covered the remaining tribes who were not part of his kingdom when he was anointed king the first time at Hebron.

The association between recognizing David as king and the anointing can be seen in one encounter that David had with a group of men who wanted to join him. 1 Chronicles 12:18 says:

> Then the Spirit came upon Amasal, chief
> of the Thirty, and he said: "We are yours,

O David! We are with you, O son of Jesse!
Success, success to you, and success to those
who help you, for your God will help you."

Amasal's anointing occurred in the same moment that he rec-
ognized David as his king.

The anointing oil poured out from a horn was purified
by a sacrificial death, but the anointing oil itself—the part of
the anointing that actually touched the priest-king—carried
its own consecrating power. According to Exodus 30:23-25,
the anointing oil was to be composed of 500 shekels of liquid
myrrh and cassia and half as much cinnamon and fragrant cane,
all mixed in with a hint of olive oil, which was the delivery
agent. The myrrh, which is associated with the suffering and
death of Jesus, was used in burials and purification ceremonies
and to deaden pain. It was one of the spices brought to Jesus
by the wise men as a foreshadowing of His death. A mixture
of it with wine was offered to Jesus while on the cross, and it
was one of the spices that anointed His body when He was
put in the tomb. The resin was extracted from the wounding
of a small, thorny tree—the resin being the blood of a tree.
The cassia and cinnamon, which were made from bark, the

skin of the trees, were stripped from the trees and then dried and pounded into a powder. All of the spices being produced from the wounding of trees, a symbol of the cross in the Bible.

These substances that accompanied suffering produced a scent intoxicating to people. The fragrance of the cinnamon was associated with passionate love, capturing in its essence the all-consuming desire to draw near to God and to serve Him. The myrrh was bitter to taste but produced a cleansing, pungent odor, while the cassia yielded its own sweet smell. All three ingredients were mixed into the olive oil, representing the Holy Spirit in its clear, golden essence. Those anointed were purified by the myrrh-like qualities produced by the suffering and death of Christ, poured out from a sacrificial vessel, the purification delivered through the olive oil. As they were anointed, the aroma of a life laid down and a life filled with a passionate desire to know God engulfed them. They breathed in the scent as the fluid rolled down their heads. The anointing oil did something more than purify a person who was set aside for God. The fragrance from the anointing oil became the scent of those anointed. It was absorbed into their skin and clothes, causing them to give off the aroma of a life laid down, one filled with passion for God. The anointing was more than physical; it was a physical representation of something spiritual. Ezekiel 36:26 says, "I will give you a new heart and put a new spirit in you...And I will put my Spirit in you."

The anointing of one person, the priestly king in Psalm 133, also resulted in those under his authority being anointed all separately and yet through one vessel. This is what enabled the unity promised in Psalm 133 to exist among God's people: all were anointed with the same anointing that carried with it the power to change them into people who gave off the aroma of a life laid down but also cojoined them together in one organic whole. The gifts and offices of the Holy Spirit as well as the spiritual authority and power of the Godhead were carried and dispersed through the clear golden essence of the olive oil, the Holy Spirit, God's intelligence and wisdom, seen in the way the gifts were dispersed.

The Tabernacle of David was different from the Tabernacle of Moses. While the Tabernacle of Moses was divided into the Outer Court with the brazen altar and brazen laver; the Holy Place with the Table of Showbread, the Golden Lampstand, and the Golden Altar of Incense; and the Holy of Holies with the Ark of the Covenant, the Tabernacle of David had no divisions. Under David, there was no curtain separating the ark from those who ministered before God: the Tabernacle of David itself was, in effect, the Holy of Holies. The sacrifices and cleansing that took place in the Outer Court of the Tabernacle of Moses were accomplished through the sacrificial animal that provided the anointing horn, the anointing oil itself and the one time burnt and fellowship offerings. The Levites who ministered before the Ark of the Covenant and the worshippers were not anointed in a separate ceremony like the high priest who served in the Tabernacle of Moses. Their anointing came through David, their ordination into the priesthood probably completed by the sacrifices made by David when the ark was moved to Mount Zion.

The Tabernacle of David had no Golden Altar of Incense or Golden Lampstand. First Chronicles 16:4 reveals that after the ark was installed in his tent, David "appointed Levites to minister before the ark of the Lord, to make petition, to give thanks and to praise the Lord, the God of Israel." There was no altar of incense in the Tabernacle of David because the Levites and their petitions were the incense. The Golden Lampstand in the Tabernacle of Moses lightened the darkened interior of the Holy Place, while the Holy of Holies, where the ark dwelt, had no lampstand. It was lighted with the Shekinah Glory of God (Exodus 40:34-35).

Some of these men who ministered before the tabernacle were more than musicians who composed inspired songs. In Psalm 83, Asaph prophesied of a coming plot against Israel by Edom, the Ishmaelites, Moab, Ammon, Philistia, and the people of Tyre joined by Assyria; and in Psalm 89, Ethan prophesied that David's throne would be established forever. Heman, the grandson of Samuel, was described as a seer (1 Chron. 25:50) whose wisdom was overshadowed only by that of Solomon. Heman was the author of Psalm 88. In Psalm 87, one of the Sons of Korah revealed that Zion would include people from Cush, Babylon, Philistia, and Tyre. Clearly these men were more than musicians; they were also prophets. David's anointing that enabled these men to enter into the presence of God also came the ability to prophesy through songs.

First Chronicles 15:11 says that David "summoned Zadok and Abiathar the priests" and said to them:

> You are the heads of the Levitical families,
> you and your follow Levitical families, you

and your fellow Levites are to consecrate
yourself and bring up the ark of the Lord, the
God of Israel, to the place I have prepared
for it..."

Later in 1 Chronicles 16:39, David left them to minister before the empty tabernacle in addition to those assigned to sound trumpets and cymbals and the playing of other instruments. In doing so, David was assuming the authority to change the roles of the two men who represented the two lines of descent from Aaron—who had a claim to the position of high priest—and to reorder how God was to be worshiped. Here, David, as in his decisions as to how to move the ark and where to move it, indicated that he had assumed a role much like Moses's. He was issuing proclamations for a new dispensation. Like Moses, who, although not a member of the Aaron priesthood, offered prayers, petitions, and sacrifices for the people and was the one through whom God's instruction for the Aaronic priesthood was given, David's priesthood had authority over the Aaron priesthood.

First Chronicles 27:25-31 gives a list of all the men assigned to provide provisions. David placed Jonathan, son of

Uzziah, in charge of the storehouses in the outlying districts; Ezri, son of Kelub, in charge of the field workers; Shimei the Ramathite in charge of the vineyards; and Baal-hanan the Gederite in charge of the olive and sycamore-fig trees in the western foothills. That these men were among some of those listed implies that they were gifted with a special understanding of the areas to which they were assigned, as well as having demonstrated organizational and leadership skills.

While David was anointed as a warrior, psalm writer, musician, prophet, and overseer or administrator of the distribution of the fruit of the land, those under him assumed more limited roles, focusing on the particular position assigned to them, at times probably crossing over into adjacent areas, but also involved in worship. Those called to be defenders, led by the Mighty Men, focused on the battlefield, defended the city walls, guarded the entryways or were bodyguards, while those set apart to minister before the Lord, led by Asaph, Heman, and Jeduthun, focused on leading the worship day and night, singing songs, playing instruments, offering petitions and prayers for the people, and prophesying as the Holy Spirit moved them. Other men were assigned the role of providing substance to the king, his troops, and the priests, led by men like Jonathan, Ezri, and Shimei—all roles being necessary, all roles working together to enable the Israelites to triumph. United and yet focused, they were finally able to conquer the land. The prayers and praise released the power of God to move across the country; provisions enabled the warriors, guardians, administrators, intercessors, and worshippers to focus without distraction on their respective responsibilities, the defenders on the walls protecting the home turf and the fighters going out to confront their enemies and conquering the land. In Psalm 44:4-8 , the Sons of Korah declared, "You are my king and my God who decrees victories of Jacob. Through you we push back our enemies; through your name we trample our foes. You put our adversaries to shame. In God we make our boast all day long, and we will praise your name forever." Asaph proclaimed in Psalm 76:2–3:

> His tent is in Salem,
> His dwelling place in Zion,
> There he broke the flashing arrows,
> the shields and the swords
> and weapons of war.

While the Mighty Men fought on the battlefield, those who offered praise proclaimed their victory from Mount Zion.

The citizens of David's kingdom were not just Jewish. Among the Mighty Men were Zeleck the Ammonite, Ithman the Moabite, and Uriah the Hittite. The spiritual anointing on these men likely one of the signs to the Jews of that day that God had accepted the Gentiles into the blessings of Mount Zion. Second Samuel 15:18 reveals that six hundred Philistines had become part of David's bodyguard along with some Kerethites and Pelethites, two ethnic groups whose interests were overseen by Benaiah (2 Sam. 8:18).

David's vision for Mount Zion was not just his: it was one revealed to that entire generation. In Psalm 89:19, Ethan declared,

> Once you spoke in a vision,
> to your faithful people you said:
> "I have bestowed strength on a warrior,
> I have exalted a young man from among
> my people.
> I have found David my servant;
> with my sacred oil I have anointed him.

> My hand will sustain him;
>
> No enemy will subject him to tribute..."

Ethan made it clear that God had spoken to *all the people*. And in Psalm 89: 27, Ethan said:

> I will also appoint him my firstborn,
>
> the most exalted of the kings of the earth.
>
> I will maintain my love to him forever
>
> And my covenant with him will never fail.
>
> I will establish his line forever,
>
> His throne as long as the heavens endure.

Ethan understood that the Messiah would come from David's lineage. In Psalm 76:2, Asaph proclaimed, "His tent is in Salem, his dwelling place in Zion." Asaph, in so saying, revealed that David was not the only one to realize that Mount Zion and the Salem of Melchizedek were to be the location of the tent that contained God's ark. In Psalm 45:6, the Sons of Korah declared, "Your throne, O God, will last for ever and ever;" and later, "God, your God, has set you above your companions" and "anointing you with the oil of joy." The

Sons of Korah knew that David's throne was in some way related to God's throne and that his anointing was in some way representative of the anointing of another king who was God Himself.

In an earlier age, God had appointed judges, individuals who were to lead armies against the enemies of God's people; and in later ages, God would speak to His people through individual prophets, a few chosen men in a generation appointed in times of need. But here in David's generation, on Mount Zion, an entire generation of men and women, hundreds of individuals—all were anointed in extraordinary ways. First Chronicles 12:32 says that two hundred men from Issachar and their relatives "understood the times and knew what Israel should do," and 1 Chronicles 12:14 describes the Gadites as army commanders, "the least being 'a match for a hundred, and the greatest for a thousand.'"

In Psalm 78:2, 68 Asaph revealed:

> I will open my mouth in parables,
> I will utter hidden things, things from of old...
> The men of Ephraim, though armed
> with bows,

turned back on the day of battle;

they did not keep God's covenant

and refused to live by his law.

They forgot what he had done,

The wonders he had shown them.

He did miracles in the sight of their fathers.

But they continued to sin against the

Most High...

Then he rejected the tents of Joseph,

He did not choose the tribe of Ephraim,

But he chose the tribe of Judah,

Mount Zion, which he loved.

He built his sanctuary like the heights,

Like the earth that he established forever

He chose David his servant

And took him from the sheep pens;

From tending the sheep, he brought him

To be the shepherd of his people Jacob,

Of Israel his inheritance.

And David shepherded them with integ-

rity of heart;

with skillful hands he led them.

Asaph knew on one level that the revelations his generation understood would also be forgotten. They would be shrouded in mystery for generations of Jews.

BATHSHEBA:
THE GENTILE BRIDE

2 Samuel 23:8,34,39: "These are the names of David's mighty men...Eliam son of Ahithophel the Gilonite...and Uriah the Hittite."

1 Chronicles 27:33: "Ahithophel was the king's counselor."

2 Samuel 11: 2-5: "One evening David got up from his bed and walked around on the roof of the palace. From the roof he saw a woman bathing. The woman was very beautiful, and David sent someone to find out about her. The man said, 'Isn't this Bathsheba, the daughter of Eliam and the wife of Uriah

the Hittite?' Then David sent messages to get her. She came to him, and he slept with her. (She had purified herself from her unclearness). Then she went back home. The woman conceived and sent word to David, saying, 'I am pregnant.'"

2 Samuel 12:1-4: "The Lord sent Nathan to David. When he came to him, he said, 'There were two men in a certain town, one rich and the other poor. The rich man had a very large number of sheep and cattle, but the poor man had nothing except one little ewe lamb he had bought. He raised it, and it grew up with him and his children. It shared his food, drank from his cup and even slept in his arms. It was like a daughter to him.

Now a traveler came to the rich man, but the rich man refrained from taking one of his own sheep or cattle to prepare a meal for the traveler who had come to him. Instead, he took the ewe lamb that belonged to the poor man and prepared it for the one who had come to him."

Bathsheba was not just any young woman. Her grandfather, father, and husband were part of the military and ruling elite. Her grandfather, Ahithophel, held one of the most powerful positions in the country next to the king, that of his chief advisor. Her husband, Uriah, and her father, Eliam, were men of valor and faith, They were part of the Mighty Men, the thirty or so men so exceptional that they stood out from the thousands of ordinary soldiers, earning their right to be included in that small list of elite soldiers by their character and extraordinary feats on the battlefield.

When David sent a messenger to find out the identity of his lovely young neighbor, the messenger neither identified her father's city, family relationships, or occupation. This is because Eliam, as well as Uriah, were famous and certainly known to David. They had fought beside him while he was at Hebron, helping him establish his throne. Eliam's father, moreover, was David's chief advisor, part of his specially-chosen cabinet of one, so to speak.

Bathsheba's grandfather was from Giloh, a small village north of Hebron located in the foothills of Judah in the area where David and his band of men operated for years before he assumed the throne in Hebron. In Joshua 15, Giloh is listed as being a Canaanite village assigned to Judah. Since the Israelites struggled to take control of the country, the village may still have been Canaanite when David's reign started, thus Bathsheba's family could have been Canaanite. In the chronology of Jesus's ancestry in Matthew, she is one of four women mentioned, one being a Moabite, and the other two being Canaanites, which also seems to lend merit to her possibly being a Canaanite. Even more revealing are the absence of her grandfather's name in any Jewish genealogy in the Scriptures and her marriage to a Gentile. Her husband, Uriah, a Hittite, part of a cultural group who had formed a powerful empire just north of Israel, was probably from a small settlement of Hittites living in Palestine. He and Bathsheba's father were men devoted to David, leaders renowned for their integrity and courage, her grandfather renowned for his wisdom. Uriah was undoubtedly a convert, and probably Eliam and Ahithophel as well. Bathsheba had married an

associate of her father's, an older man, who, Nathan revealed, was devoted to her.

The story that Nathan told David about the rich man who had a large number of sheep and the poor man who had nothing but an ewe lamb had details likely not randomly added but that paralleled real life. He had "bought" her, probably referring to a dowery that had been a costly sacrifice for him. Nathan made it clear that this lamb had a special relationship to the poor man, had shared his food and even drank from his "*cup*." Nathan's wording implied that Uriah had not just shared food with her—the ewe lamb had drunk from his personal cup. This implied that Uriah had shared substance deeply personal to him; he had shared spiritual food and drink with Bathsheba.

The ewe lamb, Nathan said, was like a daughter to the man of little means. Since Bathsheba's biological father was an associate of Uriah, the use of the term *daughter* in that context seems to suggest that Uriah might have been the one who opened Bathsheba's eyes to the spiritual significance of Mount Zion. This would make him her spiritual father in a sense, much as Paul called the Corinthians his children and himself their father (1 Cor. 4:14-17). And since the truth of

Scripture often abides across multiple dimensions, Uriah may also have watched her grow up as well, his relationship with her father having probably continued over many years. He was her spiritual father, but he was older and had also watched her develop into an adult.

Since no mention is made of a second wife or children in the story of Bathsheba and Uriah (individuals whom David would have been compelled to support upon Uriah's death) and Nathan's story implies that the poor man had nothing but an ewe lamb, Nathan's reference to the lamb growing up with the poor man's children may imply that Uriah had fathered a small group into Mount Zion—fellow Canaanites, perhaps. Certainly, his not spending the night with Bathsheba upon his return from war indicates that he was aware of the self-denial required of a spiritual leader, while the deference he showed David indicates that he understood spiritual authority. Nathan's revelation that Uriah was willing to share meals and spiritual knowledge with Bathsheba and others along with his assuming the role as a military leader, taking his place on the battlefield, and revealing a willingness to die for a people not his own are all marks of a Christ-like character. But in addition to his character, Uriah being included among the Mighty Men meant that he had a spiritual anointing that gave him supernatural strength along the lines of Samson and valor like that of Gideon. He had an anointed gifting in addition to the self-denying character that identifies a spiritual leader. So the children spoken of by Nathan could have been spiritual rather than literal children. Words used in the Word of God are never careless. They are there for a reason. Each word that Nathan spoke added layers to the significance of what David had done.

Nathan's use of the term *ewe lamb* suggests that Bathsheba was undoubtedly young, perhaps a teenager, causing her husband to feel protective of her. The story implies that Uriah loved her, that she was special to him.

The use of the term ewe lamb also seems to suggest that she was not at fault for what happened. Even more revealingly, the ewe lamb was slaughtered to satisfy the appetite of the wealthy man and his mysterious guest, the guest perhaps a reference to Satan, who the Scriptures say visited David on one other occasion (1 Chron. 21:1). Just as Jesus was tempted from the top of the temple by Satan, David was tempted from the top of his palace as he looked down over his stronghold and the land around it. It is implied that David had no feelings for Bathsheba and that, moreover, she was destroyed by what happened.

God often disciplines by putting the perpetrator on the receiving end of his sin, as he did with Jacob. Genesis 27-29 says that Jacob deceived his father, who was blind, into believing he was his older brother Esau by wearing Esau's clothes and covering his arms with goatskins. Years later, Jacob was on the receiving end of deception when Jacob's future father-in-law, Laban, tricked him into consummating a marriage with his firstborn, Leah, instead of Rachel by sending Leah into the marriage tent where under the cover of darkness, Jacob mistook her for Rachel. Like Jacob, David was forced into being on the receiving end of trauma like that he had inflected on others. Second Samuel 13:1-23 says that David's son Amnon lusted after his half-sister Tamar and tricked David into sending her to him on the pretext of being ill and wanting food served by her hand. Tamar, in obedience to her father, prepared food for her half-brother only to be overcome and raped. Through this heart-breaking event, God forced David as a father to experience the anguish and shame from a young woman's perspective. The lamb imagery Nathan used to describe Bathsheba also could be used to describe the obedient and unsuspecting Tamar. Bathsheba may have been about the same age as Tamar and, also like her, could have been responding naively to a summons by her king.

The fact that Nathan seemed to know intimate details about Bathsheba's and Uriah's relationship and assumed that David would not be able to deny the truth of his story implied that accuracy was hidden in the details. Also Nathan's knowledge of intimate details and assumption of David's knowledge of them furthermore implied that Uriah's and Bathsheba's relationship was well-known to the small community of five hundred to seven hundred people living in Jerusalem.

David's betrayal of Uriah was an intimate one. Upon learning of Bathsheba's pregnancy, he sent for Uriah, spoke to him, gave him a gift, and even invited him to dine with him. Finding that he was unable to persuade Uriah to visit his wife, David sent Uriah back to the army carrying back with him a letter that contained instructions for his own murder.

What happened between David and Bathsheba was a turning point for her family. While her father's name appears on the list of the Mighty Men in 2 Samuel 23:24-39, it is not on the second list in 1 Chronicles 11:11-47, although Uriah appears in both, implying that names were not removed when someone died. This also suggests that while her father didn't turn traitor, he at some point could not continue in his position as a fighting man among the Mighty Men, and dropped out of their ranks. David's messenger who identified Bathsheba used the present tense with her father, suggesting that he was alive at that time, and since their names are used together, closely associated with Uriah fighting in the field when events unfolded. Eliam must have dropped out of the ranks of the Mighty Men after Uriah had died and Bathsheba had married David. Her grandfather must have also abandoned his position as David's counselor because years later, Absalom knew that he was living in Giloh and that his relationship to David was troubled, which suggested that he might be available to join his rebellion. Perhaps Ahithophel had broken off his relationship with his granddaughter since his decision to leave Jerusalem made close interaction unlikely. Or perhaps he thought that since David's oldest sons were now men who had assumed roles as royal advisers (2 Sam. 8:18) and thus had developed powerful court alliances, his much younger great-grandchildren, representing only four of David's nineteen sons along with the additional disadvantage of their mother being guilty of an adulterous relationship

with David, were unlikely candidates for the throne. Since he could have continued as David's counselor but did not, his joining Absalom's rebellion could not have been a play to gain power. Revenge may likely have been the motive. He wanted to humiliate David in the same way that David had humiliated his family. Ahithophel accepted Absalom's invitation to join the rebellion to unseat David.

In 2 Samuel 16:20-23, Ahithophel's first advice to Absalom was strange. He wanted Absalom to lie with his father's concubines in a manner so that all of Israel would know about it. His reasoning to Absalom was that all of Israel was to be aware that David felt repulsion toward his own flesh—the results placing David in the same emotional position in which Ahithophel had been. So, a tent was pitched on the roof of the palace, and Absalom raped each of David's ten concubines in turn, their screams probably heard for blocks around the palace. Ahithophel's need for revenge made his advice useless and even detrimental to the furtherance of Absalom's rule as a legitimate king. This was not a pagan nation. For a cultural group raised under the principles of the Jewish law, incest was an abomination. Moreover, Ahithophel's words to Absalom implied that he was fully aware of this fact.

Later, having achieved his revenge, and having realized that in doing so, his famed wisdom was tarnished, and that retribution was coming, Ahithophel returned to his home in Glioh and committed suicide.

Bathsheba must have felt one psychological blow after another— the guilt over betraying an honorable man who loved her tenderly; clinging to her first born as his life drained away; watching her father disintegrate from the once-strong man of faith, a national leader of renown, and her grandfather, one of the most powerful men in the kingdom, renouncing his position, moving away, turning traitor, and then committing suicide; reliving the shame again when David's concubines, who she probably knew, were raped by Absalom upon the advice of her grandfather; her name and family's reputation dragged through the mud of scandal because of something she did while living in a culture where the sexual purity of women was of paramount importance, and having to explain all of it to her children, sons, no less. But while her father and grandfather had lost their ability to believe in the vision of Mount Zion, she overcame the pain, continued to honor David, the man who was the source of her family's downfall, and believe that God was establishing through

David something that would be a blessing for mankind. Without the emotional support of a one-on-one relationship with a husband, her relationship with David changing as more women were added to his harem, and without the support of a close-knit family, she found and maintained her emotional and spiritual balance and did not allow jealousy and unbridled ambition to set her sons against one another or against their half-brothers. She raised her children alone—one son, at least— demonstrating a love and knowledge of God and an understanding of politics, a son who became one of the wisest men of his generation and who, when he ascended the throne, demonstrated an emotional maturity well beyond his years. In Proverbs 1:8, Solomon wrote that a mother's teachings should not be abandoned, "They are a garland to grace your head and a chain to adorn your neck." In so saying, Solomon revealed that he revered his mother's wisdom. She, like her grandfather before her and her son after her, had an anointing of wisdom.

God loved David, but he also loved Uriah. In the detailing of Jesus's bloodline in Matthew, Bathsheba is not mentioned by name. Instead, Uriah's name is inserted, a man who never had an ancestral line in the Scriptures to follow him, someone who was a Gentile convert, an outsider, but who nonetheless fought for and believed that what he was doing was somehow laying a foundation for God's kingdom. Uriah's name is mentioned in the long line of humanity that led to the birth of Jesus. Matthew 1:6 simply say that "Solomon's mother had been the wife of Uriah." Uriah's name inserted rather than Bathsheba's on one level suggests that he was perhaps the reason that she first came to believe in the vision of Mount Zion and, thus, found her way into the genealogy. He was her spiritual father who had laid a foundation in her life. Certainly two of the Gentile names included, Rahab and Ruth, are mentioned because of their faith and character and not necessarily just because they were part of the bloodline; thus in mentioning Uriah, God was also throwing light on his Christ-like character. While Rahab and Ruth's spiritual ancestry began with them since they as individuals decided to leave behind their hereditary culture in order to join Israel, Bathsheba's began with Uriah. Her father and grandfather turned back while she continued to build on her foundation probably laid by Uriah. Bathsheba, who undoubtedly grieved over the role she played in Uriah's untimely death, would probably have been pleased, even comforted to see his name so honored. More importantly, in including his name, God honored a man who had loved Him, but in remembering him, God also reminded humanity that His Son, the one who was appointed to be king and to intercede on their behalf as high priest, in his role as ruler also carried the shame of sin in the DNA of his own flesh. God understood that David was doomed to failure because God's kingdom on earth could only be established through a sinless man who could wrestle with Satan and sin and overcome both. David's flawed moment only revealed just how glorious and necessary it was for the Son of God to take human form.

Matthew is the gospel that reveals Jesus as king, so Matthew 1:1 opens by revealing his place in the royal lineage, "A record of the genealogy of Jesus Christ the son of David, the son of Abraham." Matthew was stating that the foundation of Jesus's kingship did not start with David or Adam but with Abraham. The promises to Abraham were that he was to have descendants who were as numerous as the stars in the heavens and the sands of the earth and that through his seed, mankind was to be blessed. Abraham was to have both spiritual and biological children and was to be the father of all who had faith. David, it says, was a "son of Abraham," the promise of his kingdom built on the promises to Abraham that included both Jews and Gentiles and was based on faith. The Gentiles listed in the genealogy of Jesus Christ—Tamar, Rahab, Ruth, Uriah, and the wife of Uriah (Bathsheba)— indicate that Matthew was thinking about the fulfillment of those promises to Abraham and that they were deliberately mentioned as a partial fulfillment of the kingdom of Jesus Christ including both Gentiles and Jews.

David, like Jesus, had inevitable encounters with Satan. The adversary must have felt the tremors in his kingdom and, of course, showed up. But breaking through the wall of praise and the army of angelic hosts around Mount Zion took time. For an angel who was by design intended be a funnel for praise, praise must have been a penetrating weapon. In the end, what Satan thought was a victorious defeat of God's kingdom only laid a foundation for what was to come later because David's failure only revealed the necessity of a king who was sinless. David's sin revealed the glory of God's plan based on the incarnation of the Son of God. But it was through David— through his failure—that the lineage that would lead to God's kingdom would be established. As with the crucifixion where Satan thought he was victorious, God turned Satan's apparent victory into something more glorious. By establishing the royal

lineage through David and Bathsheba, God was declaring His kingdom would be peopled with a redeemed humanity, including both Jews and Gentiles, wrapped in His Holiness. The Gentiles, embodied by Bathsheba, were brought into the household of the Jewish faith.

MOUNT ZION

Acts 15:12–20: "The whole assembly became silent as they listen to Barnabas and Paul telling about the miraculous signs and wonders God had done among the Gentiles through them. When they finished James spoke up: 'Brothers, listen to me. Simon has described to us how God at first showed his concern by taking from the Gentiles a people for himself. The words of the prophets are in agreement with this, as it is written:

'After this I will return and rebuild David's fallen tent. Its ruins I will rebuild, and I will restore it, that the remnant of men may seek the Lord, and all the Gentiles who bear my name, says the Lord, who does these things that have been known for ages.'"

Hebrews 13:15: "Through Jesus, therefore, let us continually offer to God a sacrifice of praise—the fruit of lips that confess his name. And do not forget to do good and to share with others, for with such sacrifices God is pleased."

Hebrews 12:22: "But you have come to Mount Zion, to the heavenly Jerusalem, the city of the living God. You have come to thousands upon thousands of angels in joyful assembly, to the church of the first-born, whose names are written in heaven."

Mount Zion was a small city by modern standards. Situated on the eastern hill of present-day Jerusalem with the Kidron Valley on one side and Mount Moriah above it, it was approximately one-tenth of a mile wide and less than one-third of a mile long, eleven to twelve acres. Within that small space, David built his palace and something like five hundred to seven hundred people lived, according to Hillel Geva of the Hebrew University of Jerusalem[4]; and it was there that David pitched a tent for the ark.

With the establishing of the Tabernacle of David on Mount Zion, something extraordinary happened between the Jewish people of that generation and God. While the generation who encountered God at Mount Sinai remained at the bottom of the mountain gazing up at a remote and terrifying God, the generation at Mount Zion dwelled on the mountaintop with God. While the earlier generation had been separated from the throne of God on earth—the ark, by a veil—David's generation had access to God enthroned on a mercy seat. God's throne on earth was established through the work of the cross and the resurrection of Jesus, as evidenced by the rod of Aaron (the cross) which had budded (returned to life) contained inside the ark.

There is a great mystery here. This was a love relationship between God and the church. The authority of humankind on the earth re-established through the work of the cross; God reigning in the re-generated hearts of men and women.

---

[4] Shanks, H. (May/June 2016). "Ancient Jerusalem", Retrieved from https://www.biblicalarchaeology.org/daily/biblical-sites-places/jerusalem/ancient-jerusalem

In a city of fewer than seven hundred people, dedicated musicians represented a significant portion of the population. According to 1 Chronicles 25, David appointed 288 musicians in preparation for the temple. They were divided into twenty-four courses (1 Chron. 25:8-31), enough divisions to cover each hour of the day with each division composed of twelve musicians. First Chronicles 16:37 says "David left Asaph and his associates before the Ark of the Covenant of the Lord to minister there regularly, according to each day's requirement," so it can be assumed that the pattern of worship established when the Tabernacle of David was first put in place was the same—a symbolic number of musicians, probably twelve, being appointed for each hour of the day.

In order to accommodate that many musicians along with some Levites, continually offering prayers and petitions and as well as large numbers of worshipers in addition to also allowing for a respectful space where all could see the ark as well as dance, the Tabernacle of David itself must have spanned at least a quarter acre, located on at least a half-acre of land. In a city of just twelve acres, the presence of the tabernacle, as well as David's palace, must have commanded a significant portion of the city's land resources. David's tabernacle

was for an assembly and not just a few priests, as was the case with the Tabernacle of Moses.

With one division of praise and worship musicians in the tabernacle pouring forth songs and music each hour of the day, while the other twenty-three divisions of musicians and singers practiced both individually and in groups in scattered locations throughout the city, their preparation not just musical but also needing them to be spiritually attuned to God, the twelve acres of Mount Zion must have been permeated with songs of praise and thanksgiving during the day. And at night, as the normal activities of the city grew still, songs and music could still be heard pouring forth from the tabernacle against a blanket of silence. The number of psalms David wrote indicate that the king was often in their midst. David's son Solomon, who 1 Kings 4:32 says composed 1,005 songs, probably benefited from having been raised in this environment. Indeed, the lifeblood of Mount Zion was worship, their whole society revolving around it, the city filled with a sense of awe, the presence of God felt throughout the city.

After taking possession of Mount Zion and the installation of the Tabernacle of David, David's army began to take control of Israel. First Chronicles 18:1-16 and12-13 says:

In the course of time, David defeated the Philistines and subdued them, and he took Gath, and its surrounding villages from the control of the Philistines. David also defeated the Moabites, and they became subject to him and brought tribute. Moreover, David fought Hadadezer king of Zobah, as far as Hamath, when he went to establish his control along the Euphrates River. David captured a thousand of his chariots, seven thousand charioteers and twenty-thousand foot soldiers. He hamstrung all but a hundred of the chariot horses.

When the Arameans of Damascus came to help Hadadezar king of Zobah, David struck down twenty-two thousands of them. He put garrisons in the Aramean kingdom of Damascus and the Arameans became subject to him and brought tribute...Abishai son of Zeruiah struck down eighteen thousand Edomites in the Valley of Salt. .He put garrisons in Edom and all the Edomites became subject to David. The Lord gave David victory everywhere he went.

But as David gradually established his throne—before he was accepted as king of Judah, after he reigned in Hebron, and later as his authority extended to all of Israel, his conquest was different from the one that took place under Joshua. His was a kingdom with the major thrust of the battle taking place in the spiritual realm. First Chronicles 14:14–15 says about the battle to re-take Baal Perazim that God told David:

> As soon as you hear the sound of marching in the tops of the balsam trees, move out to battle, because that will mean God has gone out in front of you to strike the Philistine army.

David did not just gain control over the land—people switched allegiance. First Chronicles 14:12 says that after the first battle for Baal Perazim, the Philistines abandoned their gods there. Later, 2 Samuel 15:18 provides evidence as to just how profoundly changed the Philistines and Canaanites were by their encounters with David's army. The Scriptures reveal that when David fled from Absalom, six hundred Philistines from Gath, the former city of Goliath were found among his bodyguard, in addition to Kerethites and Pelethites, other ethnic groups that dwelt in Israel. When David encouraged the Philistine leader Ittal to return and serve Absalom, he refused to leave David's side (2 Sam. 15:18-22). They were intensely loyal to David, and, consequently, David had come to trust them with his life. Ittal was more than a servant; David later put him in authority over a third of his troops. The Kerethites and Pelethites, also among David's personal bodyguard, were not part of a conquered people who were controlled by military garrisons. Second Samuel 8:18 says David had appointed someone from his administration, Benaiah, to look after their interests. Under David, Gentiles served in the military but were also part of the government. Ahithophel the Gilonite was David's chief advisor. There is every indication that these Gentiles were more than politically loyal; their being included in David's kingdom seemed to be based on faith. Obed-Edom, a Philistine in whose house the ark was once housed, became a gatekeeper for the ark. Second Samuel 24:21 and 22 says Araunah the Jebusite addressed David as 'my king' and hoped that God would accept David's sacrifice, implying an understanding of the need for sacrifice. Uriah the Hittite was a man of faith.

In Psalm 87, the Sons of Korah sang about those "born" in Zion who were from Babylon, Philistia, Tyre, and Cush. Those individuals who were born in Zion had a second birth, the first being the one that defined their ethnicity as being a Philistine or a Babylonian.

> He has set his foundation on the
> holy mountain;
> the Lord loves the gates of Zion more
> than all the
> dwellings of Jacob.
> Glorious things are said of you, O city of God:
> > "I will record Rahab and Babylon among
> > those who acknowledge me---Phillistia
> > too and Tyre, along with Cush---
> and will say, 'This one was born in Zion.'
> Indeed, of Zion it will be said,
> 'This one and that one was born in her,
> and the Most High himself will establish her.

> The Lord will write in the register of
> the peoples:
> 'This one was born in Zion.'
> As they make music they will sing,
> 'All of my fountains are in you.'"

The book of Psalms, fruit of the Tabernacle of David, was a revelation of a new way of worship for the people of God. Even Moses's song Psalm 90, his priesthood, and way of worship anticipating David's tabernacle is included because his way of worship belonged to the same type of worship. And Psalm 72, composed by Solomon, whose life overlapped the Tabernacle of David, can also be said to be a representation of this form of worship. The key to God's power and presence being released for that generation lay in this new form of worship: adoration of God with musical instruments and voices, hands lifted up in an act of surrender and adoration, and even dancing, as David did when he brought the ark onto Mount Zion. As Psalm 149:3 says: "Let them praise his name with dancing and make music to him with tambourine and harp." Worship brought the Kingdom of Heaven to earth, joining together the heavenly and earthly. As Hebrews 12:22 says:

"But you have come to Mount Zion, to the heavenly Jerusalem, the city of the living God. You have come to thousands upon thousands of angels in joyful assembly, to the church of the first-born, whose names are written in heaven."

The books of wisdom—Proverbs, Ecclesiastes, and Song of Songs—written in greater part in the years that followed and composed mostly by Solomon, who was raised under the tutelage of the Tabernacle of David, represent the extraordinary wisdom and intimate understanding of God released through the Tabernacle of David. The Song of Songs was a revelation of a soul drawing near to God, while Proverbs revealed something more than God's laws; it imparted His *wisdom*. These books revealed an intimacy and an understanding of God's mind not expressed in Genesis, Exodus, Leviticus, Numbers, and Deuteronomy, the books of the Bible that existed prior to Mount Zion.

God began laying the foundation for the revelation of His kingdom with the desperate cry of a woman named Hannah, whose name means *grace*. She was the barren, second wife of Elkanah, whose name means *God has made*, from the hill country of Ephraim, which means *fertile* or *more is to come*. Hannah named her son Samuel, which means *God has heard*.

He anointed David, which means *beloved of God*, to be a king-priest in the order of Melchizedek, a foreshadowing of the priesthood of the Messiah. David was from the tribe of Judah, which means *praise*, his reign beginning with Judah and extending to all of the territory of Israel with the establishment of Mount Zion and the worship at the Tabernacle of David. The journey of the ark ended when it reached Mount Zion, the throne of God established among His people.

David's involvement with Bathsheba did not just involve adultery and murder, as bad as they are; it also, and more importantly, was a blow against the harmony and order of Mount Zion, a betrayal of the kingdom being an archetype for the Messiah and the kingdom of God. While David's grief was intense, what happened was within God's plan because the revelation of Mount Zion was only to last for one generation until the Messiah came and established His kingdom. David reigned for forty years, the designation in the Bible for one generation. God turned all of it to His and David's glory. As David's character deepened; God used the tragedy of David's flawed moment to reveal His identification with His people as sinners. Jesus's royal lineage through His mother began with the painful reality of the power of sin over humanity and the need for Jesus's sacrificial death. God wanted His people to know that their king carried in His royal lineage, in His claim to rule them, in His flesh an identity with the shame that comes with sin. David's failure also revealed that the establishment of God's kingdom on earth would require a sinless man who could confront Satan and sin and overcome both. Satan may have intended David's sin to alienate the Gentiles in David's kingdom, but God stepped around Satan's plot and established the royal bloodline through David and Bathsheba. Their marriage foreshadowed a kingdom that included both Jews and Gentiles. The Gentiles were not just outsiders who honored the Jewish god but part of the family.

The disciples spent three years and another forty days with Jesus after the resurrection. Yet with the novelty of the revelation of His kingdom so strangely new, years later, they still a struggled to understand what the details of his kingdom would look like once implemented. As the gospel of the kingdom spread to the Gentiles and they began to receive it, the apostles gathered to discuss how this revelation would be implemented in a practical way. Were the Gentiles to become Jewish converts, living according to their rules, or were their daily lives to be lived differently?

In the midst of the confusion of that meeting, Acts 15:13-21 reports that James stood up and quoted from Amos 9:11:

> After this I will return and rebuild David's
> fallen tent,
> Its ruins I will rebuild, and I will restore it,
> that the remnant of men may seek the Lord,
> and all the Gentiles who bear my name...

In the stunned silence that followed, none could say anything. Their eyes had finally been opened to the mystery of the Tabernacle of David. In that model, they understood the future of the church—how the Gentiles and Jews would exist together, how the church was to worship, and God's plan for extending His kingdom to the far reaches of the earth.

The Tabernacle of David was a revelation of the age of grace that was to begin with the establishment of the church, but it also revealed what must occur in the church for the power of God to be released. It begins when the church aligned under the authority of Christ — its authority on the earth established — is not only anointed by the power and gifts of the Holy Spirit but also encased by the mantle of Christ's self-denial, an anointing that flows over and encompasses the entire body.

With a united church and the establishment of the Tabernacle of David on Mount Zion with its sacrificial and continuous praise, the power of God can begin to move. But the full apex of its power will not be seen until the Jews are restored and when every individual is in his or her place: the mighty warriors anointed with defensive power on the forefront of the battle as spiritual forces break before them, empowered by praise and prayers, gaining footholds one step at a time, moving forward, defeating the giants of today, breaking their control over the land and people, pushing back the boundaries of God's kingdom, the sacrificial praise bringing down the walls of resistance before them, giving the residents the opportunity to encounter a God they have never known. Those anointed with wisdom offering insights into God's counsel; prophets speaking God's words to the people; gatemen protecting the entryways to the city from the enemy; and those who are to provide for practical needs anointed with an understanding of how to use God's physical provisions to achieve spiritual goals, gifted with organizational skills, assisting those who need it; the labor of the people blessed so that the needs of the poor are met; members taking their turn on the battlefield, the tabernacle, or the fields; the presence of God among them, He seated on His mercy seat in the midst of all their praise.

All of the manifestations of the Holy Spirit were equally needed for the Israelities to conquer the land. For without a presence on the battlefield, there would be no one to confront the opposing forces and claim the land as the spiritual powers weakened, but without the praise and prayers, the battles would be fought heavy-handed against a stronger enemy with less effective weapons. Praise without prophetic anointing would have dulled the razor-sharp intelligence needed to identify which weapons were to be used and the point of attack. Praise without prophetic anointing would not have been effective in protecting provisions for God's people, the continuous supplies needed for all to survive. Without anointed wisdom, the troops would not have the understanding as to where and how to engage the enemy, and the battle would be fought in confusion, making the praise less powerful. Without provisions, the structure would be weakened and less able to focus, and without the anointed leadership and their understanding of God's vision, the organization lacking direction would break down into chaos.

John opened the last book of the Bible, Revelation, with messages to seven different kinds of churches. Revelation 3:7 gives the "keys of David" to the church called Philadelphia, which was united and filled with love for one another. The passage goes on to say that God has "placed before" them "an open door that no one can shut." For a church operating under the principles of the Tabernacle of David; a church united as one body, the power of praise surrounding them and going before them; a church that shares freely with one another and the needy; a church that moves boldly onto the battlefield—to that church, God has opened a door that none can shut.

James quoted from Amos 9:11-15:

> In that day I will restore David's fallen tent.
> I will repair its broken places,
> restore its ruins,
> and build it as it used to be,
> so that they may possess the remnant of Edom
> and all the nations that bear my name,
> declares the Lord, who will do these things.

The days are coming, declares the Lord,

when the reaper will be overtaken by
the plowman

and the planter by the one treading grapes.

New wine will drip from the mountains and
flow from all the hills.

I will bring back my exiled people Israel.

they will rebuild their ruined cities and
live in them.

They will plant vineyards and drink their wine;

they will make gardens and eat their fruit.

I will plant Israel in their own land,

never again to be uprooted

from the land I have given them,"

says the Lord your God.

While it is true that from time to time, churches have come close to the model of the Tabernacle of David, Amos 9:11-15 reveals complete fulfillment cannot occur until the Jews have returned to their homeland and Israel as a nation has been reestablished. David's generation was a foreshadowing of a generation that will come after Israel has returned to its homeland. The glory of this later Tabernacle of David was to be greater than the one established by David because its king was sinless and had defeated Satan.

God revealed that Jesus was the promised king by returning to the point where the dynasty of David began and by associating Him with David's humble beginnings. In the same field where David had been attending sheep when he was called to join his family and Samuel, Luke 2:8-16 says:

> And there were shepherds living out in the fields nearby, keeping watch over their flocks by night. An angel of the Lord appeared to them, and the glory of the Lord shone around them, and they were terrified. But the angel said to them,

> "Do not be afraid. I bring you good news of great joy that will be for all people. Today in the town of David a Savior has been born to you; he is Christ, the Lord. This will be a sign to you: You will find a baby wrapped in cloths and lying in a manger."

Suddenly a great company of the heavenly host appeared with the angel, praising God and saying

"Glory to God in the highest, and on earth peace to men on whom his favor rests."

When the angels had left them and gone into heaven, the shepherds said to one another, "Let's go to Bethlehem and see this thing that has happened which the Lord has told us about."

So they hurried off and found Mary and Joseph, and the baby, who was lying in the manger.

Glossary

Ark of the Covenant

The Ark of the Covenant was built according to the instructions given to Moses on Mount Sinai (Ex. 25). It was a chest constructed out of acacia wood, 52" x 31" x 31" and covered with gold inside and out. The lid was made of solid gold, and on top were two cherubim. The area between the cherubim was called the mercy seat. Inside were the stone tablets that Moses brought down from Mount Sinai, a pot of manna, and Aaron's rod.

Eli

Eli was a high priest during the time of the judges (1 Sam. 1-4). He had two sons who, although they served with him at the Tabernacle of Moses, were evil. During a battle with the Philistines, the sons of Eli removed the ark from the tabernacle and carried it into battle, where it was captured. Upon hearing this, Eli fell off his chair and broke his neck and died.

Hittites

The Hittites were an ancient people who lived in Asia Minor. The Bible says that they were descendants of Hith, and going back far enough, thought to be of Canaan. They formed a powerful kingdom to the north of Israel, but scattered settlements also existed within Israel. Abraham bought the cave where he buried Sarah from a Hittite, and Esau married two Hittites.

King Saul

Saul, from the tribe of Benjamin, was anointed by Samuel as the first king of Israel. He ruled for probably twenty years. But he disobeyed God, and Samuel told him that God had rejected him as king. During his last battle with the Philistines, fearing that he would be captured, Saul fell on his own sword.

Nathan

A prophet during the time of David.

Mount Zion

Mount Zion is a hill in Jerusalem that today is located just outside of the Old City Walls. In ancient times, the Jebusites built a fortress there, which David conquered and made his capital.

The Philistines

The Philistines were an ancient people who lived around the coastline of the Mediterranean Sea and are mentioned in the Bible because they lived on the coast of Canaan.

Samuel

During the time of the judges, Hannah, who was barren, would go to the Tabernacle of Moses and pray fervently for children. On one occasion, Eli, the high priest, thought she was drunk and rebuked her. Realizing his mistake, he then blessed her. Upon Samuel's birth and his reaching the point of being weaned, she dedicated him to serve in the Tabernacle of Moses. Samuel later became a prophet and was the one who anointed Saul as king and then David. Two books of the Bible are named after him.

Tabernacle of Moses

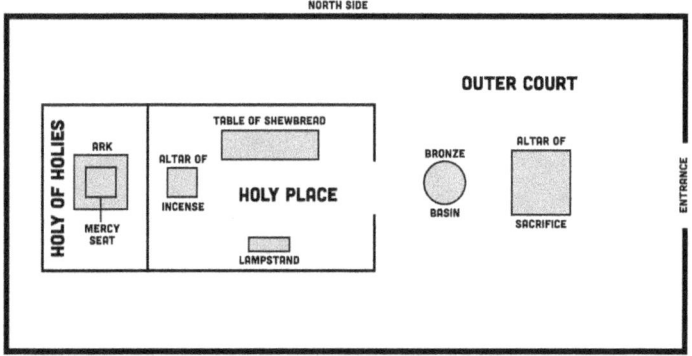

The design for the Tabernacle of Moses was given to Moses on Mount Sinai (Ex. 25-40). The Outer Court was enclosed by a linen fence and contained the Altar of Sacrifice, where the animal sacrifices were made, and the Bronze Basin, where the priest washed. The Holy Place and the Holy of Holies were in the Tent of Meeting. The Holy of Holies was separated from the Holy Place by a veil composed of four layers of curtains. The Ark of the Covenant was located in the Holy of Holies.

www.ingramcontent.com/pod-product-compliance
Lightning Source LLC
Chambersburg PA
CBHW070748110526